Exposure of Humans to Carbon Monoxide Combined With Ingestion of Diphenhydramine Hydrochloride or Phenacetin

U.S. Environmental Protection Agency

EXPOSURE OF HUMANS TO CARBON MONOXIDE COMBINED WITH INGESTION OF DIPHENHYDRAMINE HYDROCHLORIDE OR PHENACETIN

Report No.: CRC APRAC CAPM-3-68 MCOW-ENVM-CO-74-1

From the Department of Environmental Medicine, The Medical College of Wisconsin, Milwaukee, Wisconsin 53226

Supported by Contract CRC-APRAC, Project No. CAPM-3-68, from the Coordinating Research Council. Inc., and The Environmental Protection Agency

INTRODUCTION

The toxic effects of carbon monoxide (CO) have been known for many years. The exposure level, or resulting percent carboxyhemoglobin saturation (COHb), which will produce the first toxic effect, however, has become controversial.[1-4] Whatever the initial effect, the possibility of a synergistic effect of CO and commonly used drugs becomes of primary concern when establishing air quality standards.

The purpose of this investigation was to evaluate any synergistic effect of CO and two commonly prescribed drugs, phenacetin and diphenhydramine hydrochloride. Phenacetin (N-p-ethoxyphenylacetamide), an antipyretic and analgesic, is a common constituent of many proprietary pain relievers. Diphenhydramine hydrochloride (2-diphenylmethoxy-N, N-dimethylethylamine, hereafter referred to as Benadryl®) is a potent antihistaminic agent which possesses anticholinergic, antitussive, antiemetic and sedative effects. In order to discern any potential effect at levels of CO and drug doses commonly incurred, the COHb saturation tested was above average for cigarette smokers,[5] while the drug doses were those usually prescribed.[6] The results of this investigation are presented in this report.

EXPERIMENTAL PROCEDURES

Testing Procedures

During June, 1973, seven healthy male college or medical students (Table 1) volunteered for the study. The study consisted of twelve experiments run in a double blind mode to investigate the effects of CO alone, drug alone, and CO plus drug, with two replicates of each. The CO exposures were designed to rapidly raise the subjects' COHb saturation to a level of approximately 14% and then to maintain it at that level. A chronological listing of the exposures with the mean and standard deviation of the CO level and the average COHb saturation reached are presented in Table 2.

The phenacetin dosage form was prepared by grinding 300 mg tablets (Lilly) to a powder in a mortar and pestle. The powder was thoroughly mixed and weighted into individual 000 gelatin capsules on a daily basis. The dosage preparation was calculated to give each subject 10 mg phenacetin/kg body weight. The 50 mg Benadryl® (Parke-Davis) capsules were hidden in the 000 gelatin capsules with corn starch. For the no drug experiments, the gelatin capsules were filled with corn starch. As noted in the testing protocol in Table 3, drug or placebo plus a cup of water was given 5 minutes prior to entry into the environmental chamber.

Exposure Chamber

All CO exposures were carried out in the controlled environment chamber located in the Department of Environmental Medicine, The [4]

Medical College of Wisconsin. The environmental system (Carrier) provided accurate control of temperature ($72 \pm 2\,°F$) and relative humidity ($40 \pm 5\%$ RH) within the chamber, a room measuring 20 x 20 x 8 feet. The chamber was operated at a slight negative pressure with an air circulation rate of 1,200 cfm. Exhaust and make-up air capacities of 1,000 cfm provided a rapid chamber flushing capability when desired. The chamber featured pleasant lighting, comfortable chairs, individual testing carrels and a restroom facility. The subjects were under continuous visual surveillance by medical personnel while in the chamber, and in addition, their activities were visually monitored and periodically video taped by closed circuit TV (Sony).

Exposure Chamber Atmosphere

On non-exposure days, outside ambient air was flushed through the chamber. On exposure days, CO was continuously metered into the chamber's environmental system from a compressed gas cylinder in the adjacent command laboratory. Chemically pure CO with a minimum purity of 99.5% was used. The concentration of CO in the chamber atmosphere was continuously recorded from an infrared spectrophotometer (Wilks Miran I) equipped with a 20-meter path-length gas cell which was continuously flushed with air drawn from the chamber through 1/4" diameter polyethylene tubing. An MSA CO Meter and Alarm, Model 701, was also independently flushed with chamber air to provide a second independent means of continuously monitoring chamber concentration. The chamber

atmosphere was also periodically monitored by a gas chromatograph (GC)

equipped with a sequential sampler (Varian Aerograph).

All three methods of monitoring CO concentration during an exposure

were calibrated from within the chamber with standards prepared in

50 liter saran bags.

Analysis of Carboxyhemoglobin Saturation

Five-ml. aliquots of venous blood were collected in Vacutainer

tubes containing edetic acid and immediately analyzed for the hemoglobin

concentration and the percent carboxyhemoglobin saturation using a

CO-Oximeter (Instrumentation Laboratories, Inc.).

Behavioral Tests

The Flanagan Coordination Test (Science Research Associates, Inc.,

259 East Erie Street, Chicago, Illinois) measured the subject's ability to

rapidly and accurately follow a spiral pathway with a pencil. The subject,

while sitting comfortably at a desk in the individual carrel, was allowed

40 seconds to complete each of 6 spirals. The first two were considered

practice and the last four were scored and totaled. The score was determined

by the distance covered in each spiral minus the number of times the

sides of the spiral were touched with the pencil and had a maximum of 100.

The random number inspection test measured the speed with which a subject could detect the number "3" in rows of random numbers on an 8-1/2 x 11 inch page. The subject was asked to inspect each row of numbers beginning at the top of the page and mark as many 3's as possible in two minutes. The subject's score was the total number of 3's struck with a maximum score of 203 which was never achieved. Ten different pages of random numbers were used sequentially to prevent memorization of test answers.

The arithmetic test, which measured the subject's ability to work with numbers, was divided into two parts. The first part, lasting five minutes, consisted of simple addition and subtraction problems while the second part, lasting three minutes, consisted of multiplication and division. The maximum score available, if all answers were correct, was 125; however, no subject completed the test in the allotted time. In order to prevent memorization of answers, ten different tests generated from random number tables were used sequentially.

The Marquette Time Test, previously described in detail, consisted of a series of nine tone stimuli followed by a series of nine light stimuli. Each series contained stimuli of approximately 1.0, 1.5, ... 5.0 sec. duration presented in random order. At termination of each stimulus, the subject depressed a push button switch for that interval of time he estimated to be equal in duration to that of the original auditory or light stimulus. This provided a measure of his ability to estimate the duration of the stimulus; the interval between stimulus termination and onset of the response was a measure of reaction time.

The ten and thirty second time estimation tests consisted of each subject depressing the push button described above for an interval equal to that desired (10 or 30 seconds). This was repeated an additional two times for each test.

Neurological Tests

Within five minutes of entry into the environmental chamber and within 10 minutes prior to exit each subject performed a modified Romberg and heel-to-toe equilibrium test which was video taped for later inspection if necessary. The test consisted of standing upon each leg singly with arms at the side for a minimum of three seconds, and then walking a straight line heel-to-toe for approximately five feet. This was first done with the eyes open and then repeated with the eyes closed.

Electroencephalograms (EEG) and visual evoked response (VER) measurements were made on two subjects prior to and three times during each experiment. A modified 10 - 20 international electrode arrangement was used for the EEG recordings. One electrode was placed 2 to 2.5 cm.

above the inion and the VER was recorded from this electrode with the left ear as reference. The details of the recording arrangements have been published previously.[7]

The EEG and VER were both analyzed by visual examination. In addition, the amplitude of the 3rd, 4th and 5th waves of the VER complex were measured.

Clinical Testing

Each subject was given a comprehensive medical examination prior to and after the last exposure day of the study. These examinations included a complete history and physical examination with the following laboratory studies: complete blood count, SMA-12 survey panel of clinical chemistries, a 12 lead electrocardiogram (EKG), and an electro-encephalogram. Prior to each exposure, a brief physical examination was performed on each subject. At this time each subject was also questioned regarding subjective symptoms. This included questions regarding the presence of headache, eye or throat irritation, dizziness, nausea, chest pain and abdominal pain. A similar list was then taken by the subject into the chamber and each hour the subject reviewed the list for any symptoms. During the time that they were in the environmental chamber, each subject's EKG (lead II) was continuously monitored by telemetry, and recorded at hourly intervals.

Data Analysis

The data analysis of the behavioral test scores used an analysis of variance for two factors with replication. The within treatments mean square was used as the estimate of uncontrolled variability in calculating F ratios.

RESULTS: CO AND PHENACETIN

Behavioral Tests

Tables 4-14 present the mean scores for each test for each experiment, and Tables 15-25 present the analyses of variance (AOV) of these data. The AOV for the coordination test (Table 24) shows phenacetin had an effect, but, neither the CO effect nor the interaction was significant. From the mean scores in Table 17, the effect was an increase or improvement in test performance. The AOV for the arithmetic test (Table 26) shows the interaction of CO and phenacetin to be significant and Table 15 shows, from the mean scores, that again the effect was improvement of test performance.

Clinical Tests

The health of all subjects remained excellent throughout the study. The only effect which correlated with the exposures was in the subjective response list. Table 26 is a summary of the abnormal subjective responses.

When CO was administered solely, headaches occurred after 1 or 2 hours. When phenacetin was administered solely, headaches developed within 1/2 hour and ameliorated within 1/2 hour. When both CO and phenacetin were administered, headaches developed throughout the exposure beginning within 1/2 hour.

Neurological Tests

There was no discernible difference between the subjects' ability to perform the modified Romberg test or the heel-to-toe test when under the influence of CO and/or phenacetin at this exposure and dose level.

Presented in Figures 1-4 are a portion of the EEG recordings of subject 154 on four different days. Three hours of CO exposure (Figure 7) and phenacetin ingestion only (Figure 8) did not alter the EEG from baseline conditions. However, when CO exposure was coupled with phenacetin ingestion, the amplitude of the EEG was increased from baseline during both replicates (Figures 9 and 10).

There were no effects of any treatment combination in either replicate on the VER wave amplitude, latency, or configuration in either subject. The absence of amplitude alterations is illustrated in Figures 11 and 12

CO AND BENADRYL®

Behavioral Tests

Tables 27-37 present the mean scores for each test for each experiment, and Tables 38-48 present the analyses of variance (AOV) of these data. The AOV for the 10-second estimations (Table 38) shows Benadryl® had an effect, but, neither the CO effect nor the interaction was significant. From the mean scores in Table 27, the effect is found to have been a decrease in time estimation. The AOV for the Marquette Test, light stimulus, Estimate/Stimulus (Table 43) shows Benadryl® had a significant effect which, from Table 32, was an increase in time estimation or the opposite of the effect on the 10-second estimations. The AOV for the coordination test (Table 46) shows Benadryl® had a significant effect which, from Table 35, was an increase or improvement in test performance. The AOV for the arithmetic test shows Benadryl® and the interaction with CO both had significant effects which, from Table 37, were increases, or improvements, in test performance.

Clinical Tests

The health of all subjects remained excellent throughout the study. The only effect which correlated with the exposures was in the subject response list. Table 49 is a summary of the abnormal subjective responses. Benadryl® when administered produced drowsiness in the subjects which commenced within 1 hour after taking the drug and light-headedness which commenced within 2-3 hours after taking the drug. When CO was administered, headaches also commenced 1/2 - 1 hour into the exposure.

Neurological Tests

There was no discernible difference between the subjects' ability to perform the modified Romberg test or the heel-to-toe test when under the influence of CO and/or Benadryl® at these levels.

There were also no significant changes in either EEG wave frequencies and amplitude or in the VER wave amplitude, latency or configuration. The only exception to this was subject 155 who during one Benadryl® ingestion (Figure 13, upper left) had a reduced amplitude of the VER. During the second ingestion of Benadryl® he did not have an altered VER.

DISCUSSION

Behavioral Tests

Neither of these drugs combined with or without CO had significant effects on the behavioral tests. The F values from the analysis of variance which were significant appear random in nature. After phenacetin ingestion, both the coordination test and arithmetic test showed improvement in test performance. After Benadryl® ingestion, the 10 second estimations showed a decrease in time estimations, whereas, 30 second estimations did not. Also, the Estimate/Stimulus parameter for the Marquette Test was significant for the light stimulus but not for the sound stimulus. If these effects were real, the effects should have also occurred with the other parameters cited.

The improvement in test performance of the coordination and arithmetic tests following the administration of phenacetin and Benadryl® was not an unexpected result as these tests have the longest training curve of the battery of tests and, unfortunately, the experimental order was not randomized so that training and treatment effects could be examined individually.

Neurological Tests

The recordings of the cortical electrical activity were made under carefully controlled conditions. In addition, several recordings were made on every subject each day and each condition was replicated. As a result, adequate evaluations were made on each subject during each condition. The primary limitation of this study was the small number of subjects studied. Consequently, these findings serve primarily as a probe or as a base for a comprehensive study.

In our previous studies, no EEG changes were noted at COHb saturation levels of $10 \longrightarrow 15\%$. The observed change in subject 151 of this study could be an indication of intersubject variability of EEG sensitivity to the effects of CO, or to a difference in experimental procedure. As noted previously, the change in subject number 151 did not occur during this experiment but during a subsequent one where only CO was being administered but under a different protocol. Also, whereas previously no changes in the EEG were noted at COHb saturation levels of 10-15%, these levels were reached over a period of 2 ⟶ 4 hours, not 20 minutes. Therefore, the changes observed could possibly be due to the body's inability to adapt to such a fast rise in COHb saturation.

The EEG changes in subjects 151 and in 154 following phenacetin ingestion and CO exposure is classically explained as being cortical depression. However, we cannot explain why the supposed depression was not also manifested in appropriate VER changes.

The minimum COHb saturation required to produce EEG or VER changes is not well defined in the literature. Several authors have found no change in spontaneous activity of even severely poisoned animals.[8, 9, 10] Several others have found no change in human spontaneous EEG's with up to 33% COHb.[7, 11, 12] However, augmented occurrence of slow wave components in the spontaneous EEG of workers chronically exposed to 100 ppm CO was found by one investigator[13] and another found a decreased amplitude of the alpha activity at a COHb of 29%.[14] The average of COHb saturation for each experiment in this study is presented in Table 2.

Subjective Responses

A COHb saturation of 14% succeeded in eliciting headaches in 5 of the 6 subjects after 1 to 3 hours into the exposure which lasted for 1 to 4 hours. Phenacetin also elicited headaches within 1/2 hour but the headaches ameliorated within 1/2 hour. Interestingly, although an analgesic, phenacetin did not affect the headache produced by the CO exposure when both phenacetin ingestion and CO exposure were combined. The occurrence of headaches at this COHb level was also interesting as in all previous work at this laboratory, CO induced headaches did not occur until a COHb saturation of 16-18% was reached. As noted above in the EEG discussion, this could be due to intersubject variability and/ or the rapid rate which the COHb level was reached.

CONCLUSION

At drug dosages normally prescribed for phenacetin and Benadryl®, there were no synergistic effects at COHb saturations commonly experienced by heavy smokers. Three additional interesting observations were made: (1) the occurrence of CO induced headaches at COHb saturations of 14%, (2) the possible effect of CO exposure on EEG activity at this level, and (3) the finding that phenacetin, as an analgesic, did not lessen the headaches induced by the CO exposure.

ACKNOWLEDGEMENTS

The authors gratefully acknowledge the technical assistance of D. Crespo, M.D., D. Fleischfresser, S. Graff and K. Kujawski. The authors also thank Ms. Susan Kamke for her help in preparation of this

manuscript.

REFERENCES

1. Beard, R. R., Wertheim, G. A., "Behavioral Impairment Associated with Small Doses of Carbon Monoxide", Am. J. Public Health, 57:2012-2022, 1967

2. Beard, R. R., Wertheim, G. A., "Behavioral Manifestations of Carbon Monoxide Absorption", 16th International Congress on Occupational Health, Tokyo, 1969

3. Stewart, R. D., et al., "Experimental Human Exposure to Carbon Monoxide", Arch. Environ. Health, 21:154-164, 1970

4. Stewart, R. D., et al., "Effect of Carbon Monoxide on Time Perception", Arch. Environ. Health, 27:155-160, 1973

5. "Normal Carboxyhemoglobin Levels of Blood Donors in the United States", Final report to the Coordinating Research Council and the Environmental Protection Agency by the Department of Environmental Medicine, The Medical College of Wisconsin, Report # ENVIR-MED-MCW-CRC-COHb-73-1

6. "Isolation and Identification of Drugs", Edited by E. G. C. Clarke, The Pharmaceutical Press, London, 1969

7. Hosko, M. J., "The Effect of Carbon Monoxide on the Visual Evoked Potential in Man", Arch. Environ. Health, 21:174-180, 1970

8. Lewey, F. H. and Drabkin, D. L., "Experimental Chronic Carbon Monoxide Poisoning of Dogs", Amer. J. Med. Sci., 208:502-511, 1944

9. Lindgren, S. A., "A Study of the Effect of Protracted Occupational Exposure to Carbon Monoxide with Special Reference to the Occurrence of So-called Carbon Monoxide Poisonings", Acta. Med. Scand. 167, Suppl. 356, 1-135, 1961

10. Lindenberg, R., et al., "An Experimental Investigation in Animals of the Functional and Morphological Changes from Single and Repeated Exposure of Carbon Monoxide", paper presented at AIHA Conf., Washington, D. C., 1962

11. Zorn, H., "A Contribution to the Diagnosis of Chronic CO Intoxication", Med. Indust., 33:325-329, 1964

12. Shul'ga, T.M., "New Data For Hygiene Evaluation of CO in Air", U.S.S.R. Literature, 9:73-81, 1964

13. Grudzinska, B., "Electroencephalographic Patterns in Cases of Chronic Exposure to Carbon Monoxide in Air", Folia Med. Cracov, 5:493-515, 1963

14. Sluijter, M.E., "The Treatment of Carbon Monoxide Poisoning by Administration of Oxygen at High Atmospheric Pressure", Progr. in Brain Res., 24:123-182, 1967

FIGURE 1

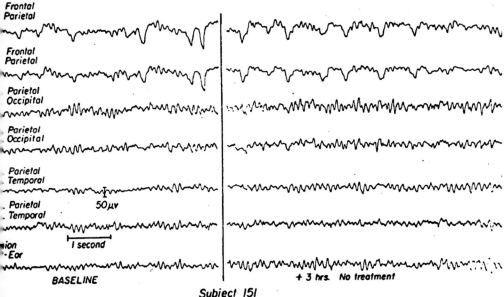

Frontal
Parietal

Frontal
Parietal

Parietal
Occipital

Parietal
Occipital

Parietal
Temporal

Parietal
Temporal

50μv

1 second

ion
Ear

BASELINE   + 3 hrs. No treatment

Subject 151
5/31/73

FIGURE 2

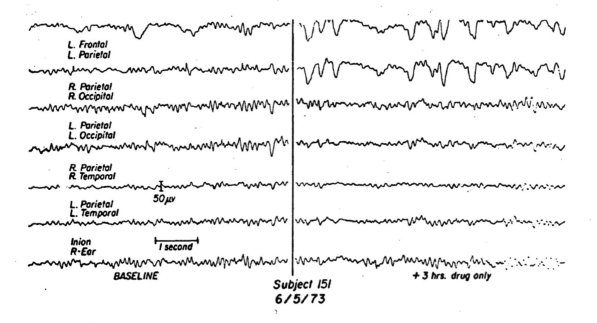

L. Frontal
L. Parietal

R. Parietal
R. Occipital

L. Parietal
L. Occipital

R. Parietal
R. Temporal

50μv

L. Parietal
L. Temporal

Inion
R-Ear

1 second

BASELINE

+ 3 hrs. drug only

Subject 151
6/5/73

FIGURE 3

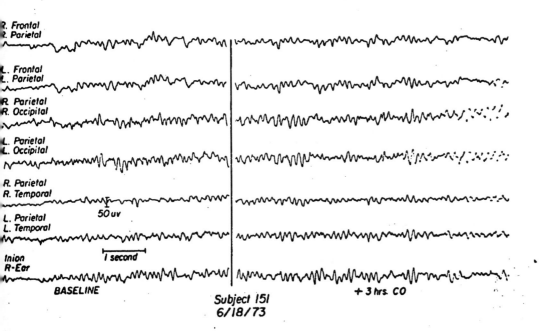

R. Frontal
R. Parietal

L. Frontal
L. Parietal

R. Parietal
R. Occipital

L. Parietal
L. Occipital

R. Parietal
R. Temporal

50 uv

L. Parietal
L. Temporal

Inion
R-Ear

1 second

BASELINE

+ 3 hrs. CO

Subject 151
6/18/73

FIGURE 4

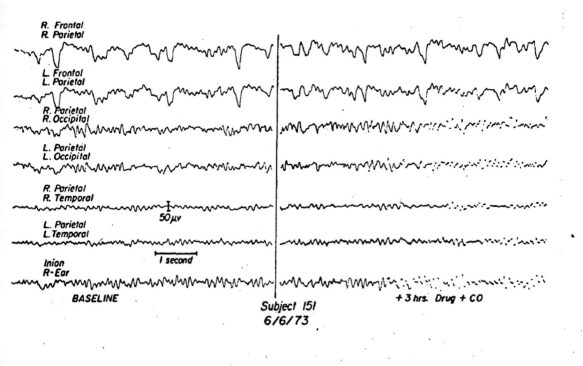

R. Frontal
R. Parietal

L. Frontal
L. Parietal

R. Parietal
R. Occipital

L. Parietal
L. Occipital

R. Parietal
R. Temporal

50 μv

L. Parietal
L. Temporal

1 second

Inion
R-Ear

BASELINE

Subject 151
6/6/73

+ 3 hrs. Drug + CO

FIGURE 5

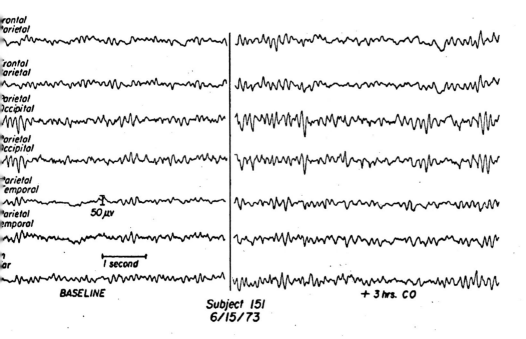

BASELINE

50 μv

1 second

+ 3 hrs. CO

Subject 151
6/15/73

FIGURE 6

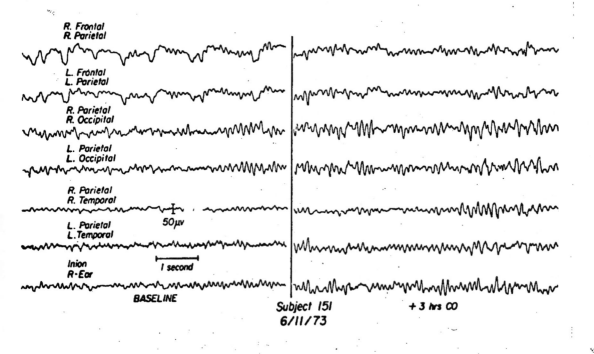

R. Frontal
R. Parietal

L. Frontal
L. Parietal

R. Parietal
R. Occipital

L. Parietal
L. Occipital

R. Parietal
R. Temporal

50μv

L. Parietal
L. Temporal

Inion
R·Ear

1 second

BASELINE

Subject 151
6/11/73

+ 3 hrs CO

FIGURE 7

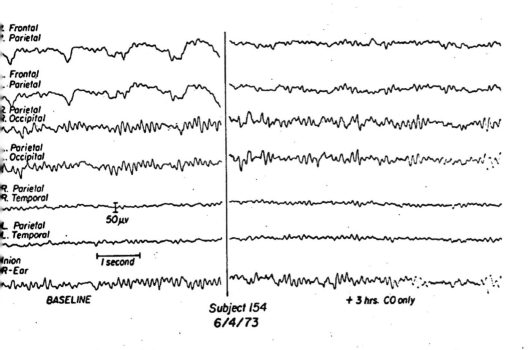

R. Frontal
R. Parietal

L. Frontal
L. Parietal

R. Parietal
R. Occipital

L. Parietal
L. Occipital

R. Parietal
R. Temporal

L. Parietal
L. Temporal

Inion
R-Ear

50μv

1 second

BASELINE

Subject 154
6/4/73

+ 3 hrs. CO only

FIGURE 8

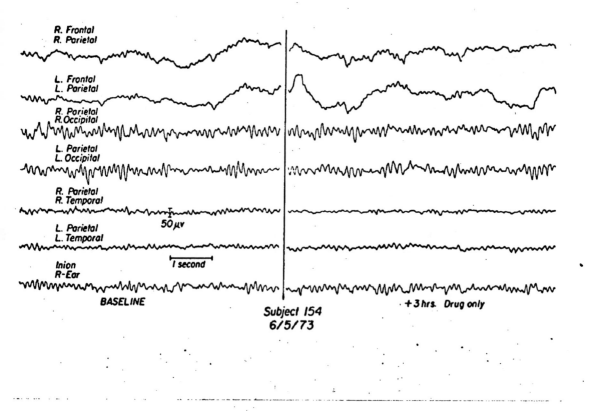

R. Frontal
R. Parietal

L. Frontal
L. Parietal

R. Parietal
R. Occipital

L. Parietal
L. Occipital

R. Parietal
R. Temporal

50 μv

L. Parietal
L. Temporal

Inion
R-Ear

1 second

BASELINE

+3 hrs. Drug only

Subject 154
6/5/73

FIGURE 9

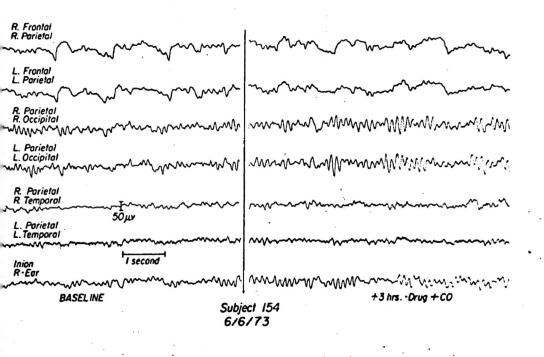

BASELINE

Subject 154
6/6/73

+3 hrs. ·Drug +CO

FIGURE 10

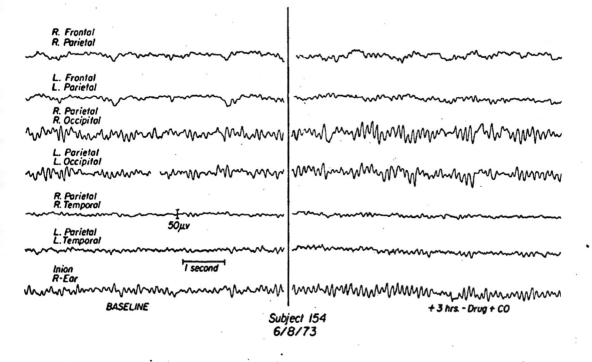

R. Frontal
R. Parietal

L. Frontal
L. Parietal

R. Parietal
R. Occipital

L. Parietal
L. Occipital

R. Parietal
R. Temporal

50μv

L. Parietal
L. Temporal

Inion
R-Ear

1 second

BASELINE

+ 3 hrs. - Drug + CO

Subject 154
6/8/73

FIGURE 11

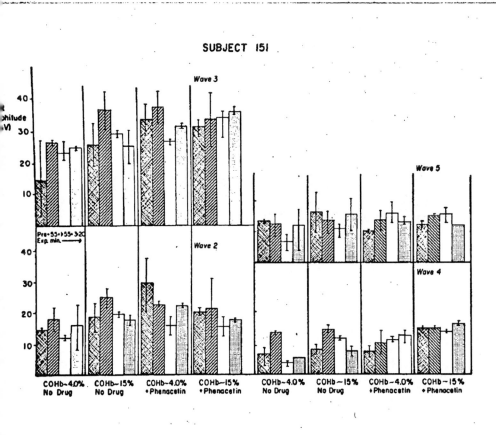

FIGURE 12

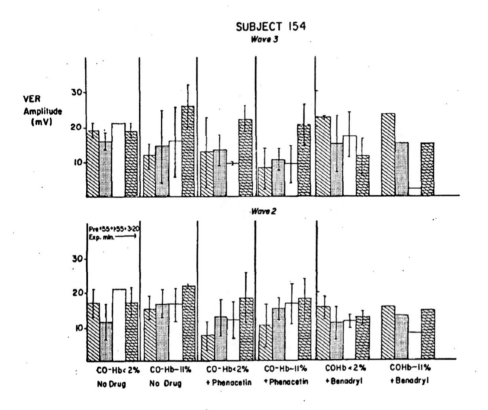

SUBJECT 154
Wave 3

VER
Amplitude
(mV)

Wave 2

CO-Hb<2%   CO-Hb~11%   CO-Hb<2%   CO-Hb~11%   COHb<2%   COHb~11%
No Drug   No Drug   +Phenacetin +Phenacetin +Benadryl +Benadryl

FIGURE 13

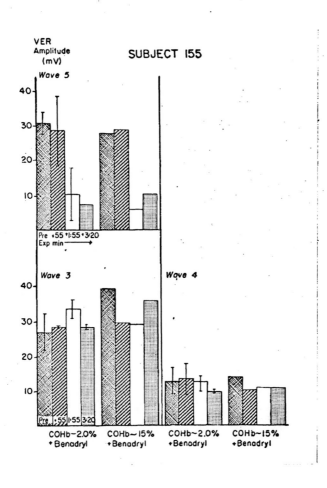

VER
Amplitude
(mV)

SUBJECT 155

Wave 5

Pre +55 +1·55 +3·20
Exp min ⟶

Wave 3

Wave 4

COHb~2.0%
+Benadryl

COHb~15%
+Benadryl

COHb~2.0%
+Benadryl

COHb~15%
+Benadryl

TABLE 1

PHYSICAL CHARACTERISTICS OF SUBJECTS

Subject	No.	Age, yrs.	Ht., cm.	Wt., kg.
K.K.	150	22	181	73.6
K.M.	151	24	177	71.3
E.S.	152	23	183	88.1
D.J.	153	25	186	78.1
I.K.	154	23	185	83.5
D.N.	155	23	180	61.4
W.F.	156	19	171	72.0
AVERAGE		22.7	180.4	75.4

TABLE 2

CHRONOLOGICAL LISTING OF EXPERIMENTS

Experiment No.	CO Concentration Mean	S. D.	Duration Hr.	Drug	Average % COHb
1	<1	--	3.5	--	1.58
2	<1	--	3.5	--	1.68
3	1,011.3 / 141.5	45.5 / 108.3	0.5 / 3.0	--	13.49
4	<1	--	3.5	Phenacetin	1.80
5	983.0 / 123.9	74.9 / 45.9	0.5 / 3.0	Phenacetin	11.36
6	<1	--	3.5	Phenacetin	0.93
7	1,001.1 / 128.1	32.8 / 81.4	0.5 / 3.0	Phenacetin	14.10
8	968.8 / 117.6	102.3 / 41.1	0.5 / 3.0	--	13.10
9	<1	--	3.5	Benadryl	1.90
10	980.0 / 104.6	91.3 / 52.1	0.5 / 3.0	Benadryl	14.78
11	<1	--	3.5	Benadryl	2.48
12	988.1 / 124.3	70.6 / 50.7	0.5 / 3.0	Benadryl	14.58

TABLE 3

PROTOCOL: CARBON MONOXIDE PLUS DRUG

C.D.T.	Elasped Time	
9:00 A.M.	-1'00"	Subjects arrive (Breakfast of 8 oz. orange juice, 2 slices toast w/butter and jam at home prior -2'30"). VER on 2 subjects (smoker and non-smoker) All subjects-physical, blood, urine, EKG and electrodes ECG strip
9:55	-0'05"	All subjects - take medication
10:00	0	All subjects - enter chamber, subjective response All subjects - Romberg & heel-to-toe
10:50	0'50"	All subjects - subjective response 2 subjects - VER
11:00	1'00"	All subjects - behavioral tests, EKG strip
11:30	1'30"	All subjects - subjective response 2 subjects - VER
11:40	1'40"	All subjects - EKG strip
1:10 P.M.	3'10"	All subjects - subjective response, blood, Romberg & heel-to-toe 2 subjects - VER
1:20	3'20"	All subjects - exit chamber, EKG strip All subjects - lunch

Subjects should have no coffee or alcohol after midnight of the night prior to the experiment. Smokers should smoke no more than 2 cigarettes in the morning prior to the experiment.

TABLE 4

THE EFFECT OF PHENACETIN AND CARBON MONOXIDE ON
10 SECOND ESTIMATIONS

		PLACEBO	10 mg/kg PHENACETIN
No CO	REP 1	10.56	9.86
	REP 2	9.86	10.84
CO	REP 1	10.10	10.28
	REP 2	10.41	10.62

TABLE 5

THE EFFECT OF PHENACETIN AND CARBON MONOXIDE ON

30 SECOND ESTIMATIONS

		PLACEBO	10 mg/kg PHENACETIN
No CO	R E P 1	30.91	30.43
	R E P 2	31.42	33.04
CO	R E P 1	30.45	32.18
	R E P 2	32.53	31.49

TABLE 6

THE EFFECT OF PHENACETIN AND CARBON MONOXIDE ON

THE MARQUETTE TEST (Estimate/Stimulus; Sound)

		PLACEBO	10 mg/kg PHENACETIN
No CO	REP 1	1.05	1.04
	REP 2	1.01	1.08
CO	REP 1	1.02	1.05
	REP 2	1.13	1.07

TABLE 7

THE EFFECT OF PHENACETIN AND CARBON MONOXIDE ON THE MARQUETTE TEST (|Estimate-Stimulus|; Sound)

		PLACEBO	10 mg/kg PHENACETIN
No CO	REP 1	0.28	0.38
	REP 2	0.36	0.43
CO	REP 1	0.35	0.34
	REP 2	0.50	0.39

TABLE 8

THE EFFECT OF PHENACETIN AND CARBON MONOXIDE ON
THE MARQUETTE TEST (Reaction Time; Sound)

		PLACEBO	10 mg/kg PHENACETIN
No CO	R E P 1	0.24	0.25
	R E P 2	0.27	0.25
CO	R E P 1	0.25	0.26
	R E P 2	0.23	0.25

TABLE 9

THE EFFECT OF PHENACETIN AND CARBON MONOXIDE ON
THE MARQUETTE TEST (Estimate/Stimulus; Light)

			PLACEBO	10 mg/kg PHENACETIN
No CO	REP 1		0.93	0.99
	REP 2		0.98	0.96
CO	REP 1		0.94	0.97
	REP 2		0.95	1.01

TABLE 10

THE EFFECT OF PHENACETIN AND CARBON MONOXIDE ON
THE MARQUETTE TEST (|Estimate/Stimulus|; Light)

		PLACEBO	10 mg/kg PHENACETIN
No CO	REP 1	0.35	0.28
	REP 2	0.31	0.36
CO	REP 1	0.41	0.35
	REP 2	0.28	0.34

TABLE 11

THE EFFECT OF PHENACETIN AND CARBON MONOXIDE ON
THE MARQUETTE TEST (Reaction Time; Light)

		PLACEBO	10 mg/kg PHENACETIN
No CO	REP 1	0.30	0.31
	REP 2	0.31	0.30
CO	REP 1	0.31	0.32
	REP 2	0.27	0.30

TABLE 12

THE EFFECT OF PHENACETIN AND CARBON MONOXIDE ON
THE COORDINATION TEST

		PLACEBO	10 mg/kg PHENACETIN
No CO	REP 1	103.86	115.57
	REP 2	106.43	114.29
CO	REP 1	111.43	115.29
	REP 2	101.38	110.86

TABLE 13

THE EFFECT OF PHENACETIN AND CARBON MONOXIDE ON
THE INSPECTION TEST

		PLACEBO	10 mg/kg PHENACETIN
No CO	REP 1	64.86	64.86
No CO	REP 2	65.28	57.29
CO	REP 1	62.00	66.14
CO	REP 2	54.88	61.71

TABLE 14

THE EFFECT OF PHENACETIN AND CARBON MONOXIDE ON THE ARITHMETIC TEST

		PLACEBO	10 mg/kg PHENACETIN
No CO	REP 1	85.86	86.00
No CO	REP 2	91.43	85.71
CO	REP 1	81.57	89.43
CO	REP 2	75.00	88.86

TABLE 15

ANALYSIS OF VARIANCE TABLE FOR THE EFFECT
OF PHENACETIN AND CARBON MONOXIDE ON 10-SECOND ESTIMATION

Source of Variation	SS	DF	MS	F
Carbon Monoxide	0.011	1	0.011	0.054
Phenacetin	0.056	1	0.056	0.269
C x P	0.001	1	0.001	0.007
Subtotal	0.069	3		
Within Treatments	0.834	4	0.208	
TOTAL	0.903	7		

TABLE 16

ANALYSIS OF VARIANCE TABLE FOR THE EFFECT
OF PHENACETIN AND CARBON MONOXIDE ON 30-SECOND ESTIMATION

Source of Variation	SS	DF	MS	F
Carbon Monoxide	0.087	1	0.087	0.059
Phenacetin	0.425	1	0.425	0.286
C x P	0.027	1	0.027	0.018
Subtotal	0.539	3		
Within Treatments	5.935	4	1.484	
TOTAL	6.474	7		

TABLE 17

ANALYSIS OF VARIANCE TABLE FOR THE EFFECT
OF PHENACETIN AND CARBON MONOXIDE ON
THE MARQUETTE TEST (ESTIMATE/STIMULUS; SOUND)

Source of Variation	SS	DF	MS	F
Carbon Monoxide	0.001	1	0.001	0.433
Phenacetin	0.000	1	0.000	0.077
C x P	0.001	1	0.001	0.498
Subtotal	0.002	3		
Within Treatments	0.008	4		
TOTAL	0.010	7		

TABLE 18

ANALYSIS OF VARIANCE TABLE FOR THE EFFECT OF PHENACETIN AND CARBON MONOXIDE ON THE MARQUETTE TEST (|ESTIMATE - STIMULUS|; SOUND)

Source of Variation	SS	DF	MS	F
Carbon Monoxide	0.002	1	0.002	0.502
Phenacetin	0.000	1	0.000	0.040
C x P	0.010	1	0.010	2.539
Subtotal	0.013	3		
Within Treatments	0.016	4	0.004	
TOTAL	0.029	7		

TABLE 19

ANALYSIS OF VARIANCE TABLE FOR THE EFFECT
OF PHENACETIN AND CARBON MONOXIDE ON
THE MARQUETTE TEST (REACTION TIME; SOUND)

Source of Variation	SS	DF	MS	F
Carbon Monoxide	0.000	1	0.000	0.102
Phenacetin	0.000	1	0.000	0.139
C x P	0.000	1	0.000	1.128
Subtotal	0.000	3		
Within Treatments	0.001	4		
TOTAL	0.001	7		

TABLE 20

ANALYSIS OF VARIANCE TABLE FOR THE EFFECT
OF PHENACETIN AND CARBON MONOXIDE ON
THE MARQUETTE TEST (ESTIMATE/STIMULUS; LIGHT)

Source of Variation	SS	DF	MS	F
Carbon Monoxide	0.000	1	0.000	0.092
Phenacetin	0.002	1	0.002	4.273
C x P	0.000	1	0.000	0.626
Subtotal	0.003	3		
Within Treatments	0.002	4		
TOTAL	0.005	7		

TABLE 21

ANALYSIS OF VARIANCE TABLE FOR THE EFFECT
OF PHENACETIN AND CARBON MONOXIDE ON
THE MARQUETTE TEST (|ESTIMATE - STIMULUS|; LIGHT)

Source of Variation	SS	DF	MS	F
Carbon Monoxide	0.001	1	0.001	0.292
Phenacetin	0.000	1	0.000	0.014
C x P	0.000	1	0.000	0.002
Subtotal	0.001	3		
Within Treatments	0.013	4	0.003	
TOTAL	0.014	7		

TABLE 22

ANALYSIS OF VARIANCE TABLE FOR THE EFFECT
OF PHENACETIN AND CARBON MONOXIDE ON
THE MARQUETTE TEST (REACTION TIME; LIGHT)

Source of Variation	SS	DF	MS	F
Carbon Monoxide	0.000	1	0.000	0.176
Phenacetin	0.000	1	0.000	0.668
C x P	0.000	1	0.000	0.469
Subtotal	0.000	3		
Within Treatments	0.001	4		
TOTAL	0.001	7		

TABLE 23

ANALYSIS OF VARIANCE TABLE FOR THE EFFECT
OF PHENACETIN AND CARBON MONOXIDE ON
THE COORDINATION TEST

Source of Variation	SS	DF	MS	F
Carbon Monoxide	0.172	1	0.172	0.011
Phenacetin	135.375	1	135.375	8.397*
C x P	4.875	1	4.875	0.302
Subtotal	140.422	3		
Within Treatments	64.484	4	16.121	
TOTAL	204.906	7		

*Significant, $P < .05$

TABLE 24

ANALYSIS OF VARIANCE TABLE FOR THE EFFECT
OF PHENACETIN AND CARBON MONOXIDE ON
THE INSPECTION TEST

Source of Variation	SS	DF	MS	F
Carbon Monoxide	7.133	1	7.133	0.446
Phenacetin	1.117	1	1.117	0.070
C x P	45.039	1	45.039	2.818
Subtotal	53.289	3		
Within Treatments	63.941	4	15.985	
TOTAL	117.230	7		

TABLE 25

ANALYSIS OF VARIANCE TABLE FOR THE EFFECT
OF PHENACETIN AND CARBON MONOXIDE ON
THE ARITHMETIC TEST

Source of Variation	SS	DF	MS	F
Carbon Monoxide	25.008	1	25.008	2.681
Phenacetin	32.578	1	32.578	3.493
C x P	93.070	1	93.070	9.979*
Subtotal	150.656	3		
Within Treatments	37.305	4	9.326	
TOTAL	187.961	1		

*Significant, $p < .05$

TABLE 26

Recorded Abnormal Subjective Responses for CO and Phenacetin

Exp. #	CO	DRUG	IMMEDIATE	1/2 HOUR	1 HOUR	2 HOUR	3 HOUR
1	N	N	-	-	-	-	-
2	N	N	-	-	-	-	-
3	Y	N	-	-	headache (152)	headache (151, 153)	-
4	N	Y	-	headache (155, 156)	-	-	-
5	Y	Y	-	headache (153)	headache (153)	headache (151)	headache (152, 154)
6	N	Y	-	drowsy (155)	-	-	-
7	Y	Y	-	headache (153)	headache (153)	headache (152, 153)	headache (152, 153)
8	Y	N	-	-	-	headache (153)	headache (151, 152, 153) (154, 155, 156)

Subject numbers given in parenthesis

-56-

TABLE 27

THE EFFECT OF BENADRYL AND CARBON MONOXIDE ON
10 SECOND ESTIMATIONS

		PLACEBO	50 mg. BENADRYL
No CO	R E P 1	10.56	9.30
	R E P 2	9.86	9.81
CO	R E P 1	10.10	9.37
	R E P 2	10.11	9.02

TABLE 28

THE EFFECT OF BENADRYL AND CARBON MONOXIDE ON
30 SECOND ESTIMATIONS

		PLACEBO	50 mg. BENADRYL
No CO	R E P 1	30.90	30.99
No CO	R E P 2	31.42	30.31
CO	R E P 1	30.45	29.09
CO	R E P 2	32.27	29.46

TABLE 29

THE EFFECT OF BENADRYL AND CARBON MONOXIDE ON
THE MARQUETTE TEST (Estimate/Stimulus; Sound)

		PLACEBO	50 mg. BENADRYL
No CO	R E P 1	1.05	1.20
	R E P 2	1.01	1.18
CO	R E P 1	1.02	1.11
	R E P 2	1.16	1.11

TABLE 30

THE EFFECT OF BENADRYL AND CARBON MONOXIDE ON

THE MARQUETTE TEST (|Estimate-Stimulus|; Sound)

		PLACEBO	50 mg. BENADRYL
No CO	R E P 1	0.28	0.62
	R E P 2	0.36	0.51
CO	R E P 1	0.35	0.41
	R E P 2	0.55	0.45

TABLE 31

THE EFFECT OF BENADRYL AND CARBON MONOXIDE ON

THE MARQUETTE TEST (Reaction Time; Sound)

			PLACEBO	50 mg. BENADRYL
No CO	R E P 1		0.24	0.28
	R E P 2		0.27	0.22
CO	R E P 1		0.25	0.24
	R E P 2		0.26	0.24

TABLE 32

THE EFFECT OF BENADRYL AND CARBON MONOXIDE ON
THE MARQUETTE TEST (Estimate/Stimulus; Light)

		PLACEBO	50 mg. BENADRYL
No CO	R E P 1	0.93	1.04
No CO	R E P 2	0.98	1.08
CO	R E P 1	0.94	1.09
CO	R E P 2	0.96	1.03

TABLE 33

THE EFFECT OF BENADRYL AND CARBON MONOXIDE ON
THE MARQUETTE TEST (|Estimate-Stimulus|; Light)

		PLACEBO	50 mg. BENADRYL
No CO	REP 1	0.35	0.43
	REP 2	0.31	0.40
CO	REP 1	0.41	0.33
	REP 2	0.31	0.37

TABLE 34

THE EFFECT OF BENADRYL AND CARBON MONOXIDE ON
THE MARQUETTE TEST (Reaction Time; Light)

		PLACEBO	50 mg. BENADRYL
No CO	REP 1	0.30	0.35
No CO	REP 2	0.31	0.27
CO	REP 1	0.31	0.35
CO	REP 2	0.31	0.32

TABLE 35

THE EFFECT OF BENADRYL AND CARBON MONOXIDE ON
THE COORDINATION TEST

		PLACEBO	50 mg. BENADRYL
No CO	REP 1	103.86	115.75
No CO	REP 2	106.43	123.00
CO	REP 1	111.43	121.25
CO	REP 2	112.87	124.00

TABLE 36

THE EFFECT OF BENADRYL AND CARBON MONOXIDE ON
THE INSPECTION TEST

		PLACEBO	50 mg. BENADRYL
No CO	REP 1	64.86	64.25
	REP 2	65.29	54.50
CO	REP 1	62.00	60.25
	REP 2	59.22	52.25

TABLE 37

THE EFFECT OF BENADRYL AND CARBON MONOXIDE ON
THE ARITHMETIC TEST

		PLACEBO	50 mg. BENADRYL
No CO	REP 1	85.86	86.25
	REP 2	91.43	94.00
CO	REP 1	81.57	101.50
	REP 2	82.71	100.25

TABLE 38

ANALYSIS OF VARIANCE TABLE FOR THE EFFECT
OF BENADRYL AND CARBON MONOXIDE ON 10-SECOND ESTIMATION

Source of Variation	SS	DF	MS	F
Carbon Monoxide	0.109	1	0.109	0.999
Benadryl	1.225	1	1.225	11.250*
C x B	0.032	1	0.032	0.293
Subtotal	1.366	3		
Within Treatments	0.436	4	0.109	
TOTAL	1.802	7		

*Significant, $P < .05$

TABLE 39

ANALYSIS OF VARIANCE TABLE FOR THE EFFECT
OF BENADRYL AND CARBON MONOXIDE ON 30-SECOND ESTIMATION

Source of Variation	SS	DF	MS	F
Carbon Monoxide	0.693	1	0.695	1.331
Benadryl	3.348	1	3.348	6.407
C x B	1.236	1	1.236	2.366
Subtotal	5.279	3		
Within Treatments	2.090	4	0.522	
TOTAL	7.369	7		

TABLE 40

ANALYSIS OF VARIANCE TABLE FOR THE EFFECT
OF BENADRYL AND CARBON MONOXIDE ON
THE MARQUETTE TEST (ESTIMATE/STIMULUS; SOUND)

Source of Variation	SS	DF	MS	F
Carbon Monoxide	0.000	1	0.000	0.105
Benadryl	0.015	1	0.015	5.393
C x B	0.010	1	0.010	3.688
Subtotal	0.026	3		
Within Treatments	0.011	4	0.003	
TOTAL	0.037	7		

TABLE 41

ANALYSIS OF VARIANCE TABLE FOR THE EFFECT
OF BENADRYL AND CARBON MONOXIDE ON
THE MARQUETTE TEST (|ESTIMATE - STIMULUS|; SOUND)

Source of Variation	SS	DF	MS	F
Carbon Monoxide	0.000	1	0.000	0.002
Benadryl	0.023	1	0.023	3.117
C x B	0.036	1	0.036	4.839
Subtotal	0.059	3		
Within Treatments	0.030	4	0.007	
TOTAL	0.089	7		

TABLE 42

ANALYSIS OF VARIANCE TABLE FOR THE EFFECT
OF BENADRYL AND CARBON MONOXIDE ON
THE MARQUETTE TEST (REACTION TIME; SOUND)

Source of Variation	SS	DF	MS	F
Carbon Monoxide	0.000	1	0.000	0.066
Benadryl	0.000	1	0.000	0.347
C x B	0.000	1	0.000	0.143
Subtotal	0.000	3		
Within Treatments	0.002	4		
TOTAL	0.002	7		

TABLE 43

ANALYSIS OF VARIANCE TABLE FOR THE EFFECT
OF BENADRYL AND CARBON MONOXIDE ON
THE MARQUETTE TEST (ESTIMATE/STIMULUS; LIGHT)

Source of Variation	SS	DF	MS	F
Carbon Monoxide	0.000	1	0.000	0.012
Benadryl	0.023	1	0.023	25.507*
C x B	0.000	1	0.000	0.023
Subtotal	0.023	3		
Within Treatments	0.004	4	0.001	
TOTAL	0.027	7		

*Significant, P< .01

TABLE 44

ANALYSIS OF VARIANCE TABLE FOR THE EFFECT
OF BENADRYL AND CARBON MONOXIDE ON
THE MARQUETTE TEST (|ESTIMATE - STIMULUS|; LIGHT)

Source of Variation	SS	DF	MS	F
Carbon Monoxide	0.001	1	0.001	0.176
Benadryl	0.003	1	0.003	1.539
C x B	0.005	1	0.005	2.283
Subtotal	0.008	3		
Within Treatments	0.008	4		
TOTAL	0.016	7		

TABLE 45

ANALYSIS OF VARIANCE TABLE FOR THE EFFECT OF BENADRYL AND CARBON MONOXIDE ON THE MARQUETTE TEST (REACTION TIME; LIGHT)

Source of Variation	SS	DF	MS	F
Carbon Monoxide	0.000	1	0.000	0.376
Benadryl	0.001	1	0.001	0.569
C x B	0.000	1	0.000	0.180
Subtotal	0.001	3		
Within Treatments	0.004	4		
TOTAL	0.005	7		

TABLE 46

ANALYSIS OF VARIANCE TABLE FOR THE EFFECT
OF BENADRYL AND CARBON MONOXIDE ON
THE COORDINATION TEST

Source of Variation	SS	DF	MS	F
Carbon Monoxide	52.531	1	52.531	6.110
Benadryl	305.391	1	305.391	35.520*
C x B	7.047	1	7.047	0.820
Subtotal	364.969	3		
Within Treatments	34.391	4		
TOTAL	399.359	7		

*Significant, $P < .005$

TABLE 47

ANALYSIS OF VARIANCE TABLE FOR THE EFFECT
OF BENADRYL AND CARBON MONOXIDE ON
THE INSPECTION TEST

Source of Variation	SS	DF	MS	F
Carbon Monoxide	26.937	1	26.937	1.310
Benadryl	53.090	1	53.090	2.582
C x B	0.586	1	0.586	0.029
Subtotal	80.613	3		
Within Treatments	82.234	4	20.559	
TOTAL	162.848	7		

TABLE 48

ANALYSIS OF VARIANCE TABLE FOR THE EFFECT
OF BENADRYL AND CARBON MONOXIDE ON
THE ARITHMETIC TEST

Source of Variation	SS	DF	MS	F
Carbon Monoxide	9.023	1	9.023	0.768
Benadryl	204.313	1	204.313	17.394*
C x B	148.805	1	148.805	12.668*
Subtotal	362.141	3		
Within Treatments	46.984	4	11.746	
TOTAL	409.125	7		

*Significant, $P < .025$

TABLE 49

Recorded Abnormal Subjective Responses for CO and Benadryl

Exp. #	CO	DRUG	IMMEDIATE	1/2 HOUR	1 HOUR	2 HOUR	3 HOUR
1	N	N	-	-	-	-	-
2	N	N	-	-	-	-	-
7	Y	N	-	headache (153)	headache (153)	headache (152, 153)	headache (152, 153)
8	Y	N	-	-	-	headache (153)	headache (151, 152, 15. 154, 155)
9	N	Y	-	-	drowsy (151, 154)	drowsy (151, 152, 154)	drowsy (151, 152, 15. dizzy (153)
10	Y	Y	-	-	drowsy (151)	drowsy (151, 152) dizzy (151)	drowsy (152, 153) dizzy (151)
11	N	Y	-	-	-	drowsy (151)	-
12	Y	Y	-	-	headache (151, 152, 153)	drowsy (151, 152, 153) headache (152, 153)	drowsy (151, 152, 15. headache (152, 153)

Subject numbers are given in parenthesis

CPSIA information can be obtained at www.ICGtesting.com
Printed in the USA
BVOW06s1752050214

344055BV00014B/476/P